'Pete Maidment is witty, humorous, insightful, thought-provoking and creative. I am delighted that he has taken up the challenge of producing what is decidedly, and rightly, not a confirmation course but a fabulous resource to produce brilliant confirmation preparation sessions. Read the really helpful opening chapters, then let your young people delve into the themes and ideas to help them get ready for their confirmation. They will grow, and so will the leaders. Terrific stuff!'

The Rt Revd Paul Butler, Bishop of Durham

'Getting young people ready for confirmation is a privilege and a great opportunity but it can also be a daunting task. Reading *Are You Ready?* is like sitting down with a good friend who knows just what you need to hear. Pete Maidment talks us through what confirmation is, what young people are like and how to create a tailor-made course for your group from the rich buffet that he provides in the book. Pete's love of young people and years of experience as a youth worker shine through this excellent resource – highly recommended.'

Jenny Baker, author of *Equals* and Development Manager for the Church Urban Fund

'A really impressive course. Easy to use, with minimal preparation. Flexible, imaginative . . . with a wide range of topics.'

The Revd Richard Harlow, Rector, Tadley with Pamber Heath and Silchester, Hampshire

Pete Maidment has been the Diocesan Youth Adviser for the Diocese of Winchester since 2005. Previously a youth worker for a large church in Southampton and a village parish in Surrey, he also worked with Youth for Christ in Rochdale and Portsmouth. For a short time, he was in charge of a youth centre in Woking for Surrey County Council. A published author, Pete co-wrote *Reconnecting with Confirmation* (2011) and contributed to *Young People and Worship* (2007), both published by Church House Publishing. He also co-wrote *Living Your Confirmation* (SPCK, 2012). He is married and has two children.

ARE YOU READY?

PREPARING YOUNG PEOPLE TO LIVE THEIR CONFIRMATION

PETE MAIDMENT

First published in Great Britain in 2015

Society for Promoting Christian Knowledge
36 Causton Street
London SW1P 4ST
www.spckpublishing.co.uk

British Library Cataloguing-in-Publication Data
A catalogue record for this book is available from the British Library

ISBN 978–0–281–07149–4
eBook ISBN 978–0–281–07150–0

Typeset by Graphicraft Limited, Hong Kong
First printed in Great Britain by Ashford Colour Press
Subsequently digitally printed in Great Britain

eBook by Graphicraft Limited, Hong Kong

Produced on paper from sustainable forests

For my Mum

CONTENTS

PREFACE: HOW TO USE THIS BOOK

This is the bit where I tell you who this book is for, what the book isn't and how to use the material.

WHO IS *ARE YOU READY?* FOR?

I've been working with young people since I was 19, and apart from a brief spell installing car stereos at Halfords, it's pretty much all I've ever done. I speak youth-worker.

But this book definitely isn't primarily for youth workers (although obviously I hope they'll all buy a copy . . .).

The book is aimed at those of you who, year after year, prepare young people for confirmation. It's for those who've tried all the various Christian basics courses, who've scoured the internet for the latest ideas and inspiration and, yes, who've emailed the Diocesan Youth Adviser hoping there's some new course out there that's evaded capture until now.

It's written with clergy in mind, as well as volunteer youth leaders and of course paid youth workers. The ideas are mostly simple (although there are a few crazier ones thrown in – I am a Messy Church leader after all!), and most take very little preparation. I really hope anyone who picks up the book will be able, within a few minutes, to have the outline of a session ready to go.

WHAT *ARE YOU READY?* ISN'T

I'm concerned that I may repeat this phrase over and over again, but *Are You Ready?* isn't a course as such. A course, or more accurately a curriculum, suggests that the book covers all the things you need to get done before your group can get confirmed.

This book isn't that. Rather it's a buffet of sessions and activities for you and your group to select from and to choose the bits that would most help. I've just started the course with a group myself – we're going to do three of the sessions from Part 2 of the book ('The Apostles' teaching', 'Fellowship' and 'Prayer'), then I'm going to throw it open to them to see which of the Commission sessions they'd like to do, and which of the Issues sessions (I'll explain the structure of the book in a moment). We only have six weeks together, and I'm getting to know them from scratch; plus each session is only 45 minutes long. So I'm using the material to suit that group rather than squeezing them into the curriculum that I have in front of me. In an ideal world I'd be working with a group of young people I know really well. We'd meet weekly for a couple of hours and would have a good ten weeks together. But how often do we get to operate in an ideal world?

HOW TO USE THIS BOOK

The book is divided into three parts. Part I contains some background to the material: Chapter I explores the meaning of confirmation for young people today; Chapter 2 considers what it means to be an adult Christian and the role of confirmation in a young person's journey of faith; Chapter 3 explains how the sessions work.

Part 2 has two sections. The first section – 'The Commission' – is written as a prequel to *Living Your Confirmation*, the confirmation gift book I co-wrote with Bishop Paul Butler in 2012.[1] *Living Your Confirmation* has ten chapters that walk a newly confirmed young person through the Commission from the confirmation service. The likewise ten chapters – or sessions – in this section of *Are You Ready?* include reflections and activities to help that young person engage as well as possible with the key discipleship practices he or she is going to commit to at confirmation.

The second section of Part 2 – 'Issues' – contains a set of chapters/sessions that look in detail at some common life issues your group may be facing. It's certainly not an exhaustive list but it is based on feedback from youth workers on issues they're regularly asked about, as well as my own observations. I've tried really hard to avoid the usual media hype and not be sensationalist about any of these issues; rather I've tried to help you view them from a young person's perspective.

Part 3 comprises a simple liturgy to help your group mark the start of the confirmation preparation process, as well as an outline for a pre-confirmation retreat, with a number of activities. Both are useful ways of helping your group of young people prepare for the major step they're about to take.

Above all, I view this book as a *learning* rather than a *teaching* resource. I've avoided listing 'stuff-you-ought-to-tell-your-group', opting instead for activities to encourage you and them to engage with subjects and to discover together. I think it works.

Oh and by the way: reading this preface doesn't mean you don't need to read the other preliminary chapters. Go on, turn the page . . .

ACKNOWLEDGEMENTS

Lots of people have helped me along the way as I've written this book. It's not something I could have achieved alone.

Massive thanks must go to the young people from Lord Wandsworth College who have put up with my experimenting with their confirmation preparation over the last four or five years, and to Simon Leyshon, the former chaplain there, as well as John Morris, the current chaplain, for inviting me back year after year.

I'm grateful to my family for letting me spend hours behind my computer while dust gathered and washing-up piled high. Fortunately I'm blessed with a patient wife and with children who humour me.

Finally, thank you to Tracey Messenger from SPCK who has, once again, patiently prodded and poked me, never seeming to lose her temper despite my total inability to meet any deadlines or reply to emails. What a saint!

Thank you

Pete

INTRODUCTION

'Is confirmation a ritual, a rite of passage or a sacrament?' That's the question I got asked this week, and it's galvanized me into sitting down and writing. With two books on confirmation under my belt as well as a couple of articles and several training days, the thing I've avoided time and again is trying to pen some kind of confirmation preparation course, despite the niggling feeling that I really should give it a go.

The trouble is this: I don't think it's really possible to write a curriculum for confirmation. There's no set list of things a young person or group of young people need to be educated in before they're fit for confirmation. For me confirmation preparation is a *living* thing – not surprisingly, since it's all about preparing a bunch of living things (young people) for a living ceremony confirming their faith in a living God. And so my fear all along has been that if I write a confirmation course it will become static, a set-in-stone document that denies the fact that confirmation preparation is about engaging in the real lives of young people and walking alongside them as they prepare for confirmation. This book isn't written to be that kind of course. Don't panic: you aren't going to be expected to lead your group through 19 sessions of material before they're ready to be confirmed! Rather, what I offer here is a selection of ideas and inspiration to help you and your group go on a discipleship journey together. Think of it as that huge bank of pick-and-mix sweets you get in some shops. You wouldn't ever try to eat a sweet from each of the containers. You'd choose some of your favourites, test out a couple of new ones and go away happy. That's why this opening section is so important – it sets the scene for you, the course leader, before you begin the preparation process with your group.

DOUBT AS THE CURRICULUM FOR CONFIRMATION

There are two key writers who have shaped my thoughts about the way we should prepare young people for confirmation. The first is Andrew Root, an associate professor at Luther Seminary, Minnesota. Root is a key voice in the call for a better understanding of relational ministry with young people. In 2010 he wrote an article entitled 'Doubt as the Curriculum for Confirmation', in which he calls for confirmation teachers to see the time of preparation as an opportunity to walk alongside young people and explore doubts together. Right from the outset, Root argues that we should be clear that the Christian faith is about questions, wondering, uncertainty and discomfort. Too often our confirmation preparation becomes a syllabus of 'God stuff' that we need to know in order to stand in confidence before the bishop, safe in the knowledge we've learnt all the right things. The trouble is, that's not how the vast majority of us think. How many Christians do you know who feel completely at ease with what they believe? How many are confident they've got the whole thing wrapped up? I'd guess very few, and that the ones who seem so confident are, when you scratch the surface, as angst-ridden as the rest of us! I recently led a training session for volunteer youth leaders, and partway through I confessed that my faith felt a bit rocky at the moment; that I was struggling to get my head around some of the stuff that for many years I'd held as 'gospel'. No one left the room; no one wrote to the bishop and asked for my resignation. In fact one woman looked at me and said, 'I love you!' For her, to hear that the 'person at the front' had doubts and struggles and concerns about faith was a massive relief. A really good friend of mine who's a

Christian in full-time ministry recently explained to me that for him the Christian faith existed on the cusp of belief and agnosticism. What a relief!

The funny thing about all these examples is that they all come from adults – people who've long since left the uncertainty and turmoil of adolescent development, who are individuated beings and who in terms of faith development could be described as having an 'owned faith'. And yet they have doubts and questions and concerns. Just think how much more doubt there must be for a young person who's in the middle of the fires of adolescence, who no longer has the confidence of a pre- or early adolescent able to rely on the faith of others.[1] The temptation is to see young people's doubts as risk ('They're doubting. Quick: give them some certainty so they don't lose their faith'), when actually doubt is something we need to grow comfortable with – it will accompany us for the rest of our lives.

I've often wondered about the image of faith Jesus gives us. If we only had faith the size of a mustard seed, he says, we'd be able to say to mountains: 'Move from here to there' and they would move (Matthew 17.20). While there's obviously an admonishment here of followers who have so little faith, I do sometimes wonder too if he is offering us a picture of just how low he sets the bar. Is there a lovely comic picture here? Surely we're not being asked to indulge in a little terraforming but rather being shown how little faith we need. Peter Rollins' reflection that 'to believe is human; to doubt divine' keeps me trusting in the fact that doubt isn't something to be avoided or feared.[2]

Blogger Jason Clark, commenting on David Kinnaman's book *You Lost Me*, notices that one of the key reasons for young people leaving the Church is that it isn't a safe place to doubt. More than a quarter of young people have serious doubts they'd like to discuss but don't feel they can raise because of the way their church will perceive them.[3] It may not seem like a huge percentage but, as Kinnaman notes, these aren't statistics but stories from individuals. And, of course, the numbers add up – we can be sure there are tens of thousands of young Christians who feel they're 'not allowed to talk about [their] doubts in church'.[4]

If confirmation preparation is to become a place where young people can express and explore their doubts, then it needs to be a living thing. No material I write can possibly create a space where young people can comfortably explore matters of faith. That's why this book is far more a collection of tools and ideas for you to use in building relationships and exploring faith with your group – it's not a curriculum or a syllabus you need to complete, rather a staring point with some signposts along the way.

The trouble with following a course or curriculum for confirmation preparation is that we very quickly become tied to the contents of the lovely glossy book we've shelled out our hard-earned money for. It's written down, so we have to use it! And so our sessions with young people become far more focused on completing the material than on the real purpose of our time together, which is building relationships and exploring faith. In youth-work terms, we lose sight of the *needs* of the young people in our care.

The needs of young people is a good place to start as you begin planning how you'll prepare them for confirmation. If you've bought a confirmation course because it makes it easier for you to know what to do with this group of teens, then can I humbly suggest that you may need to step back for a moment and have a bit of a think. In that case the published course in your hand is primarily meeting your need for a quiet life (which I completely understand by the way). The point is that this isn't just another group of confirmation candidates in front of you; this is a gathering of individual young people, with all sorts of passions, worries and desires, and you have the enormous privilege of joining them on this journey of faith. What you deliver over the next few weeks or hours needs to stem from their needs as developing Christians.

I'll be honest: I find confirmation classes exhausting. Regardless of how amazing the material I've written is, regardless of how mind-blowingly life-changing the message might be, at the end of the day I'm in a room full of adolescents with their own ideas, questions and musings, and sometimes it's impossible to get through. That's why at last night's session we discussed: cat breading (the act of cutting a hole in a piece of bread and putting it over your cat's head before taking a photo of it and posting it on the internet – feel free to do an online image search); that one of the boys in the groups can recite pi to 103 decimal places (which he did – to my amazement); and why in the USA no one cares if you have ginger hair. In fact the most spiritual the discussion got was when it turned out that the main reason one of the girls wanted to be confirmed was because her parents had told her that you can only get married in a church if you are.

Starting with the young people's needs should, theoretically, make the sessions much easier. Rather than trying to force them into my way of thinking, I'm discovering what they're after and then seeking to fulfil that need. Now I know that may all sound a little woolly. I told a friend I'd planned to let young people set the agenda for the next confirmation preparation, and she rather dismissively responded 'Well, Jesus won't even get a mention then.'

PRACTISING PASSION

Here we come to the second key writer who's influenced the way I think about confirmation preparation. Kenda Creasy Dean, who is Professor of Youth, Church and Culture at Princeton Theological Seminary, has written many fine books, but my favourite and the one I've seen her lecture from is *Practicing Passion*.[5] In that book she argues that young people have three main needs: acceptance; feeling part of greatness; camaraderie.

ACCEPTANCE

Young people need to feel accepted – by their culture and *primarily* by adults. Dean argues that the problem in contemporary society is that adults, whether driven by fear, apathy or busyness, are largely invisible for most young people – the majority struggle to find adults with whom they can develop strong, healthy relationships. In fact some sociologists argue that for many, adolescence simply doesn't end, meaning that there just aren't any real adults anymore for your young people to develop relationships with. (If you think that sounds ridiculous, just work out how much you've spent on toys in the last 12 months – by which of course I mean phones, tablets and the like.) The need to be accepted addresses the adolescent desire

for steadfastness, continues Dean. For many young people, Jesus' promise, 'I am with you always, to the end of the age' (Matthew 28.20), is of paramount comfort. God fulfils this need for acceptance with fidelity; young people can trust in God always to be there for them, and that trust is authenticated by an adult 'being there' for a young person. That's the first role of the confirmation leader: to be an *adult*, to be available, to be trustworthy and to be there for the group. It's why a series of get-togethers with your group, over a period of weeks, is probably the best way to prepare young people for their confirmation. It's also why your relationship with them must go beyond the service at the end of a course, otherwise the feeling will be that you simply travelled with them to get them ready for the bishop – the relationship wasn't lasting. For the last few years I've been invited to lead the confirmation preparation for a boarding school in the diocese. Initially I was sceptical about the role – it seemed a bit hit and run for my liking. Yes, I'd be there for eight weeks running, but then I'd disappear and all that work on building relationships would be lost. To my surprise, however, the relationships have proved enduring. There are young people who return to confirmation classes year after year because of the relationships we've built. One young man is about to start his fourth series of confirmation preparation but still has no plans to get confirmed. He just likes being part of the group and values the relationship. It's certainly not the ideal – I'm still absent from the school for 44 weeks of the year – but the importance of just 'being there' is proven none the less.

FEELING PART OF GREATNESS

Young people, Dean writes, have a developmental need to feel part of greatness. That's grand language. Put simply: young people want to get high. There's an adolescent desire for ecstasy. Of course, the majority of young people don't take drugs and a large number don't drink to excess, but there remains in the young an overwhelming desire for 'the other' – to be part of the big thing that takes them beyond themselves. So whether it's drugs, sex or rock and roll, young people have always had a need to get outside of themselves. If the first role of the confirmation prep leader is to model the imminence of God, the second is to make space for young people to experience the transcendence of God – to find opportunities for them to be moved.

I recently helped lead a 24/7 prayer week for a school.[6] We had a couple of assemblies and the students were given resources and ideas to create prayer spaces around the campus, but the highlight for me was the service of compline we held at the end of school halfway through the week. Being a super-trendy youth worker, I'd dubbed it 'hyper modern night prayer', but in reality it was a very simple liturgical service overlaid with video clips, music and some creative prayer activities. The service ended with some time-lapse video clips of sunsets in various beautiful locations set to music. The transcendent moment came when the music faded and the images ceased, and the silence began.

Now I'm very conscious of those quiet moments, especially when young people are involved. The last thing I want is for the quiet to feel imposed and the group to be secretly wishing they could escape, so I kept my eyes open to make sure the moment finished before boredom or embarrassment set in. I'm also conscious that young people are hungry for ecstasy and prone to 'consider *any* moving personal experience, from roller coasters to orgasms, potentially "spiritual"'.[7] The last thing I want is some hyped-up emotional experience that the young people might confuse with being spiritual. To my amazement though, this group of young people, many of whom weren't practising Christians, who'd been giggling and messing around just before, sat in absolute silence. The moment lasted. I believe we experienced something of the transcendent in that moment – we touched God, or more likely God touched us. Of course, the moment passed and needless to say the event ended with pizza, but I believe we were all changed by that experience. And the adolescent desire for ecstasy had been filled, albeit for a short while, by my willingness to create a space in which young people could be moved.

CAMARADERIE

Finally (and I guess this will come as no surprise to any of us), young people have a developmental need for camaraderie, expressed as the adolescent desire for intimacy. If asked, the majority of young people would assume that intimacy means *physical* intimacy. We live in a culture obsessed and immersed in sex, and so when young people discover this overwhelming desire for intimacy, and look at all the signals being thrown at them by the world around them, it's not surprising that so often their reaction is a physical, sexual response.

Intimacy is, of course, far more than sexual or physical. It is, explains Dean, 'being known' by someone. While young people think that what they crave is the ecstasy of physical intimacy, what underlies that desire is a hunger for communion with someone, ultimately communion with God – communion in its fullest sense of 'being one' with someone, known and knowing. 'Postmodern youth . . . are dying for . . . someone who will be there for them, someone who can draw them beyond themselves into the mystery of "we", someone who is "one" with them and therefore holds out the gift of "being known".'[8]

I model God's response to that desire when I build a relationship with a young person. Intimacy can be found through a physical, sexual relationship but more often through simply talking. Think about it: when I sit face to face with someone and talk with that person I discover the true meaning and depth of intimacy. We learn about each other, we discover what each other believes, we are changed, we gain a closeness, we become intimate.

We recently had something of a crisis meeting at work. We met to discuss a future review process, and as some of us had been badly stung by a previous one, there was a real worry that the language of review might cause concern for members of the team. To their credit the conveners of the meeting, rather than trying to get their message across, just allowed space. There was plenty of quiet, plenty of waiting, and in time it allowed us to open up and speak honestly about our concerns. We all left the meeting feeling far more confident and secure than when we'd arrived. A level of intimacy had been discovered.

Now don't get me wrong: I'm not suggesting that at the start of your confirmation classes you announce that over the next few weeks you and the group are going to get intimate. I would suggest that this may have a detrimental effect on the longevity of your ministry! But I'd let the group know that you're going to leave plenty of space for talking and listening; for asking questions and answering; for learning from and about each other.

And that's why this book mustn't be confused with a confirmation curriculum. Your goal as you walk towards confirmation with these young people must be to try to meet those needs that adolescents have for acceptance, for feeling part of greatness and for camaraderie. The book will look like a curriculum: there are activities, discussion starters, things to think about, games and pointers to video clips. There are session titles, learning objectives and even a programme to follow. But there's deliberately far more material than you'll ever need to use, more sessions than any sane person would attempt as part of confirmation preparation. And while some subjects might be exactly what your group need in order to grow in their faith, others will seem completely irrelevant.

THE TOOLS FOR THE JOB

I recently had to have some doors hung in my house. The carpenter turned up with a van full of tools and materials. He came into the house, looked at what I had and what work needed to be done, then headed back out to his van to get the things he thought he'd need. Most of what he brought stayed in the van, and of all the equipment he brought into the house, some of that remained unused too. When he discovered a problem he hadn't foreseen he nipped out to the van to get the right tool, and at one point even went off home to get something else he needed. He didn't think that because he had the tools in his box he had to use them all. He assessed the situation and used what he needed, when he needed it, to get the job done.

If you view the task ahead of you as helping young people fulfil those needs for fidelity, transcendence and communion, then this book is simply the toolbox that you need to make that happen. I hope I haven't overstressed the point![9]